1 Ranger Rick Meets The Fawns

by J. A. Brownridge

IT HAD BEEN a long hard winter and spring seemed to be very late. At last the snow was melting and patches of new green grass were beginning to appear. Once again life was coming back to Deep Green Wood.

Squirrels ran and leaped through the trees, chattering loudly as they searched for nuts they had hidden away last fall. Pudgy Porcupine waddled down the trail looking for bark blown off trees during the heavy winter storms. Everywhere animals and birds were stirring and hurrying to start their new homes.

Ranger Rick and Ollie Otter popped into a clearing just as Cubby Bear staggered in on the other side.

"What in the world is wrong with him?" asked Ollie in amazement.

"He just woke up after his long winter nap," chuckled Rick.

4

RANGER RICK'S BEST FRIENDS

HI, I'M RANGER RICK, the official conservation symbol for young members of the National Wildlife Federation, and leader of the Ranger Rick Nature Clubs. On behalf of all the animals in Deep Green Wood, welcome to our world of nature and wildlife.

White-tailed Deer

by Anne LaBastille

**Created and Produced by
The National Wildlife Federation
Washington, D. C.**

"He really looks like it's been a long, hard night," laughed Ollie.

Fall and winter winds had blown leaves into a large pile near the trees. Walking very unsteadily and yawning at almost every step, Cubby walked into the leaf pile, tripped over his own feet, and fell flat on his face.

With a gleeful shout, animals rushed from everywhere to bury poor Cubby in his pile of leaves. Cubby roared and thrashed around and leaves flew all about. The noise echoed far and wide.

"Whew," sighed Rick, "that's enough for me. We'd all better rest awhile."

"If I wasn't so hungry right now, I'd put up a better fight," said Cubby.

"Now that you mention it, I'm pretty hungry myself," said Ollie.

"Me, too," echoed all the others.

"It's been a long winter and I guess everyone is short of food," said Rick.

A worried look crossed his face.

"What's wrong, Rick?" asked Ollie.

"I just thought about something," Rick replied. "If we're hungry, I'll bet everyone else in Deep Green Wood is hungry too, including Wally Wolf. We're making such a racket that he knows where we are."

A hush fell over the clearing. Noses sniffed each breeze and sharp ears pointed toward every sound. All eyes turned in terror as a shadow crossed the trail.

"Oh, it's only Doris Deer," gasped Ollie with relief.

"That's a nice friendly greeting," laughed Doris at the edge of the clearing.

"It's not just Doris," Rick added. "She has two new young ones with her."

"Where?" asked a puzzled Pudgy Porcupine, "I don't see anyone but Doris."

"They're there all right," answered Rick. "Look very closely. The light spots on their brown coats look just like flecks of sunlight on the ground. They're very hard to see. That's called camouflage, or protective coloration."

Doris walked carefully into the clearing followed closely by her two fawns. Now everyone could see them.

All at once, a loud cry came from a tree up the trail a short distance. It was Frances Flicker and she swooped frantically into the clearing. "Wally Wolf! Here he comes! He's just around the bend in the trail!" she screamed.

No one waited for a second warning. Animals scattered in every direction, all except Doris and her two fawns. Almost on signal, the two baby deer dropped into the pile of leaves and seemed to freeze. Doris hesitated, took one last look at her young ones, then glanced up to see Wally racing down the trail.

With a flash of her white tail, Doris took off at full speed. Down the trail she went with Wally close behind. So intent was he on Doris, and so effective was their pale color, that he raced right past the defenseless baby deer and never knew they were lying there.

Out of the woods ran Doris, into a wide green meadow, twisting and turning to escape the sharp fangs of the hungry predator. Time after time, the wolf's teeth snapped at the hind legs of the speeding deer.

On the edge of the woods, Rick and Ollie were watching anxiously.

"He's trying to cut the muscle in her hind leg," worried Rick.

"If he does, it's all over," added Ollie. "That would cripple her and she couldn't run."

But Doris wasn't finished yet. Every turn and every move took Wally farther away from her youngsters. Then, when she felt they were far enough away, Doris spurted off and left the hunger-weakened wolf far behind.

"Hooray!" shouted Rick and Ollie. "She's going to be safe."

With that, they rushed back to the clearing to find the fawns still frozen in place, not moving a muscle. Soon their mother came back to get them, and again almost as if by signal they leaped up from the leaves and nuzzled her side for food, warmth, and protection.

"Nature sure is wonderful," Ollie sighed, "but I wonder why Wally didn't smell those fawns as he went by?"

"Because nature *is* pretty wonderful," answered Rick. "Baby fawns, besides being camouflaged and taught to stay motionless, are almost scentless so they're very hard for anyone to find."

"Poor Wally," laughed Ollie. "Guess he'll just have to starve to death."

"Oh, no," Rick replied. "Wally will do all right. Mostly though, he'll catch the old, crippled, or sick animals. So he does his job in keeping a balance of nature, making sure that only strong, healthy, and smart animals survive."

"That's nice to know, Rick," giggled Ollie. "What else do you know about deer?"

"Well, Ollie," answered Rick, "just read the pages that follow this and we'll both know lots more about them. Now I've got to go, so I'll see you later."

2 The Fawns' Life Begins

Swift was just ten minutes old.

Swift lay very, very still, with his eyes shut tight. He felt weak and wet. Someone was giving him a bath. A large rough tongue was smoothing and drying his cinnamon brown fur. Every part of his tiny body, which weighed just a little more than five pounds, was being cleaned.

He dozed for awhile, then opened his big brown eyes for the first time. His mother was licking his little twin sister, Silent, who lay nearby. Swift carefully stretched his thin legs and tried to stand up. He was as wobbly as you were the first time on a bicycle. But he could stand!

Now Swift was one hour old.

Weak and wobbly, the fawn is up.

The wet newborn fawn lies quietly.
Mother deer usually helps her fawn,
but this orphan must do it alone.
Back legs first, then the front!

9

Twins, protected by dappled coats, blend into leaves of the forest floor.

Soon the fawns were full and ready to sleep again.

Mother went into the woods and left Silent and Swift alone. She did not go far, just far enough away to prevent her scent from attracting predators to her fawns. For three days after birth the fawns have no body odor, so they are perfectly safe.

By instinct both twins knew they must lie still for hours. They must never make a noise nor call to each other. The white spots on their coats looked like splashes of sun and shadow on two piles of brown leaves. The fawns were so safe that a big black bear walked within ten feet and never saw them!

During the first three weeks of their lives Swift and Silent stayed quietly bedded down in the woods. Their mother visited them during the day and gave them milk. She slept close by at night. She showed them how to nibble grass, dandelions, and twigs. Mother also licked their hind legs where the scent glands are. The fawns began rubbing their legs together to give off a special smell. This way mother could easily track them through the woods if they got lost.

With their lessons learned, Swift and Silent were ready to explore the wide world.

The twins tried walking toward their mother. They were hungry but still too tiny to reach her milk bags. So, she lay down and both babies began nursing. It was their first meal.

Did you know fawns can drink as much as eight ounces of milk in less than a minute? But they don't drink that much at every feeding. Deer's milk is twice as rich and creamy as cow's milk that you drink.

3 Growing Up in The Fall

By fall, Swift and Silent had lost their spots. Can you guess how many they lost? About 300 each. The twins and their mother were changing from their bright summer fur to heavy gray winter coats.

They began to meet other deer.

One day Swift followed a large male deer, called a buck. He saw the buck swim across a pond, jump over a fallen tree seven feet high, run through a field at 30 miles per hour, and leap across a brook 25 feet wide. Swift wondered if he would

1. In early spring two little knobs or buttons appear in front of the male's ears. 2. The knobs grow into clubs covered with dark furred skin called "velvet."
3. After a few more weeks of growth the clubs branch and become antlers. 4. The velvet peels off and leaves the hard, white branched antlers.

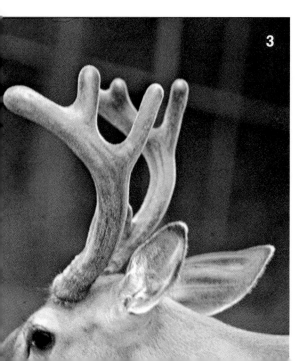

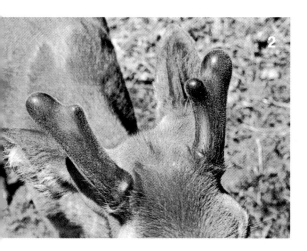

ever grow up and be able to do all those things he had just seen.

He could feel little knobs on his head, and he saw that the big buck had branching antlers growing from these knobs. He watched the buck stop by a young tree and rub the soft velvety skin off his antlers. This skin had protected the tender growing antlers all summer long. Now they were hard and sharp, so the buck scraped off the skin and made his antlers shiny. He would use these mighty weapons to fight other males and win beautiful females, called does, as his mates.

Snow fell in late November. The bucks stopped following the females. They no longer fought each other. Gradually, the antlers fell off the bucks' heads because they were not needed. It got colder and colder. A large herd of deer formed in a valley. Silent and Swift found themselves with many other half-year-olds, their mothers, and a few bucks. Other males had been killed during the hunting season. The herd huddled under thick pine trees, out of the biting wind.

Food was hard to find in the deep snow. Sometimes grownup deer would kick the twins away from little trees just as they were trying to

Bucks prepare to fight with their racks of gleaming antlers. *Below:* Cast-off antlers give hungry squirrels and other forest animals needed calcium and salt.

Silent was watching her mother closely these days. But mother had changed. No longer did she give all her attention and love to the twins. Now she spent more time with bucks who had thick necks and big racks of polished antlers. It was the fall mating season.

In the harsh days of winter, deer sometimes find it difficult to get food. Deep snow can cover all that is available.
Right: During the warm days of spring, a new fawn is born and welcomed to the family by the doe and a button buck.

reach the twigs for dinner. Many young and old deer who were not strong enough starved to death that winter. By spring, the twins were very skinny. Mother was thin, too, but her belly was large with babies.

One day in May, the mother gave birth to new fawns. She would not have much time to spend with Silent and Swift now. And Swift was growing his first little antlers. More and more he stayed alone in the woods. Silent was growing up fast, too. She would be on her own now and next year she would have a white-tailed fawn to care for and to love.

4 Deer Cousins

Along the Pacific coastal area you can find the black-tailed deer. These deer live in damp, dense forests where they can easily hide to protect themselves. There is not much to eat here. Fires and logging, however, make open places where blacktails can find tasty shrubs and young trees to browse on.

At certain times of year, blacktails may move down out of the forest to low valleys or along the ocean shore. They may lick salt off the rocks, eat seaweed, or even take a swim in the salt water. Often they swim from island to island even though the water is very cold. The farthest these deer have been seen swimming at sea is twelve miles across a rough channel. Wouldn't you think that the blacktails would be wet enough in the rainy, foggy climate of the northwestern U.S. and Alaska without going bathing in the ocean!

Branched antlers still in velvet, a black-tailed buck surveys his green kingdom.

orehead, and many-branched antlers.

MULE DEER

Out West lives the mule deer, or "mulie," with its big ears, evenly forked antlers, and short tail. These deer prefer steep mountains, open deserts, and rolling sagebrush ranges. Here they can see for long distances. They can then escape danger by running, leaping, and jumping away fast. In summer, mulies head for the high hills where insects are few and breezes are cool. Winters, they hug sunny slopes in low, sheltered valleys.

Key Deer buck and doe munch lunch on their Florida preserve. At right a buck rises to his full majestic height—29 inches at shoulder.

KEY DEER

The islands, or the keys, of South Florida shelter the tiny Key deer. This deer, the smallest in the U.S., is the size of a collie dog. They live on a few islands covered with palms, pines, palmettos and prickly pears. Often they swim across the warm, shallow waters between these islands, especially if they are chased by dogs or poachers. For years, these little deer were hunted for food and "sport" until they almost disappeared. Then conservationists began to act. Now they are safe on special Key deer refuges. Signs on the high-way warn drivers: "Caution—Key Deer Crossing."

They have little ears and a small tail. The males have antlers like the whitetails, only much smaller. When a Key deer wants to hide from danger, it lies down in a clump of prickly pears and thorny bushes where nothing can get inside to hurt it. The only thing it cannot escape is a hurricane. Sometimes these tropical storms sweep across the sea and drown the little deer. Key deer need our help so they will be safe for a long, long time.

5 Ranger Rick Finds Deer Trouble

by J. A. Brownridge

It was early in March. For a while it had seemed that winter was over, but another fierce snowstorm had swept in the night before. A deep snow blanketed the ground. Tree branches bent low under the white snow.

Ranger Rick and his buddy, Ollie Otter, had come to northern Michigan to check up on stories they had heard about deer in trouble. Rick had awakened early to take a short run by himself. Not a soul was in sight.

Just then—WHAM! A big snowball sent his hat flying into a nearby snowdrift. Before he could recover, another snowball splattered snow in his eyes, nose, and mouth.

"Whee," shouted Ollie Otter. "Two bull's-eyes with two shots!"

While Rick was gasping and trying to clear his eyes, Ollie looked out over the fields and saw two animals approaching.

"Hey, look who's coming," he called.

"That's Herman and Harry, our snowshoe hare friends," replied Rick. "Boy, look how easily they move over the snow with those big feet."

"Yes," said Ollie. "We all laugh at them in the summer. Those feet look bigger than they do. But in the snow, they can sure laugh at us. Nature provided them with built-in snowshoes."

"Hi, fellas," Herman and Harry called out together. "I'm glad you got our message because our friends the deer are really starving."

"If the deer have a food problem we'd better stop talking and get busy," said Rick. "Tell us about it on the way."

The four animals started off across country, Herman and Harry moving easily over the surface of the snow, but Rick and Ollie had to plow through it.

"We'll talk while you save your breath," laughed Herman as his two visitors struggled and gasped their way forward.

"Many people think that wildlife problems are over by now," he continued, "but look over there. See the browse line. Deer have eaten all the branches and shrubbery as high as they can reach. Now there are no branches low enough for food. With a forest fire we had last fall and the long, cold winter, there is nothing for the deer to nibble on.

"Some people put out hay, but a deer's stomach is created to digest other food and hay often doesn't work. Sometimes deer die of starvation with full stomachs! Other people put out branches and brush which deer can eat, but they put it close to roads and deer are killed by cars."

"Gosh, they do have problems," puffed Ollie.

"Yes," replied Harry, "and just over this hill, you'll see a bigger problem."

As they worked their way over the top of the hill, a strange sight met their eyes. A large herd of deer was milling around in a clearing where the snow was all trampled down.

"What's happening?" asked an amazed Ollie.

"Well, this is called a deer yard," answered Herman. "There's still a little food around here so deer from all over the area come in to try to eat. That causes more problems because they really strip the area of everything, and no one will be able to get enough to live on."

Suddenly, a piercing howl sent shivers up their spines.

"What is that?" quavered Ollie.

"Coyotes," replied Harry. "They love deer yards because so many deer in one place makes it easier for them to hunt. Some of them have probably been watching all afternoon, and now they've decided on a victim. They'll separate him from the herd and start running him."

Just then, a pair of coyotes appeared out of the woods. Slowly, they circled around an old buck that had wandered too far from the herd. Realizing his danger, the frightened deer retreated from his enemies. But every step took him farther from the safety of the herd.

Suddenly, he was completely alone. He stood bravely with antlers lowered and sharp hoofs pawing the ground. No coyote would dare make a frontal attack against those weapons. But every time the tormented deer turned, the other coyote would dash at him from the rear, snapping at his legs and stomach.

He spun, first facing one, then the other. It was clear to the watching animals that he was tiring rapidly. Then, unexpectedly, one coyote became careless and was hit by a slashing hoof. Knocked breathless, he was caught on powerful antlers and hurled through the air to land crashing in front of his companion.

Seizing his opportunity to escape, the deer raced wearily back to the herd and safety.

"Hooray!" shouted Rick and Ollie.

"Well, that one got away," said Herman, "but that doesn't happen often. The coyotes usually win. But we still haven't solved our food problem."

"No, we haven't," agreed Rick. "The main problem is that there are too many animals for this area. Whether it's cows or sheep or deer or rabbits, only a certain number of animals can get enough to eat on a given piece of land. If more are there, no one gets enough to eat; they are all hungry, weak, and ready for any disease or predator that comes along. Trained wildlife biologists consider management the answer. They try to keep a balance between the number of deer and their food and habitat. Then everyone is well fed and healthy.

"We'll head back now and ask Ranger Tom to send some people up here to study the area for a good management program. Meantime, all rangers should study what is meant by a land's 'carrying capacity.' Then they'll understand what management means, too. I hope we've all learned a lot about deer. We'll be seeing you in our next book.

"So long, everybody!"

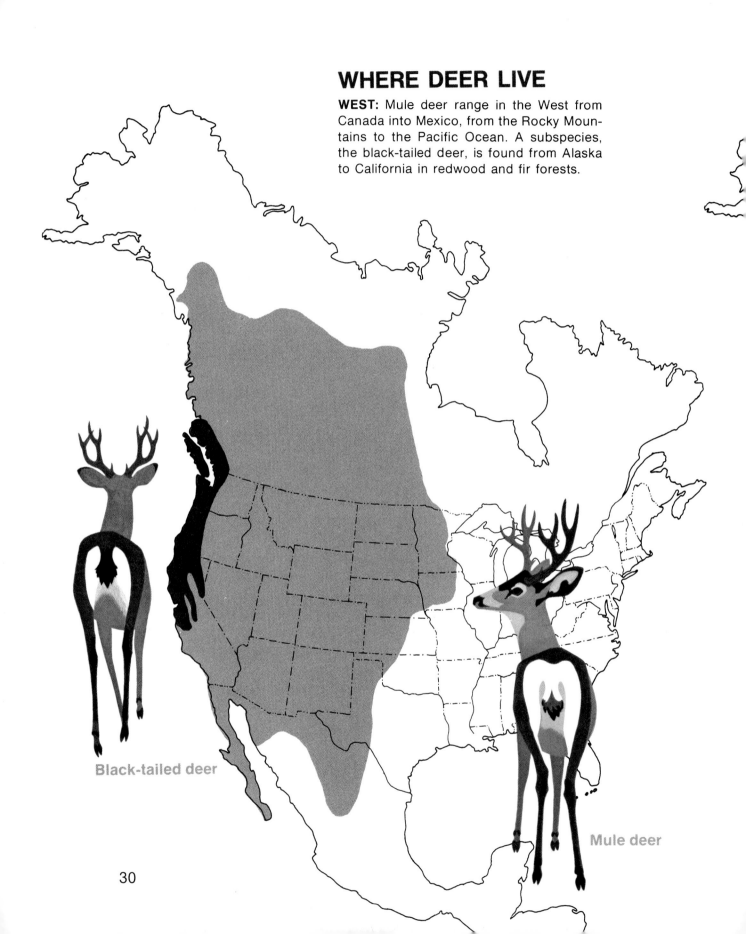

WHERE DEER LIVE

WEST: Mule deer range in the West from Canada into Mexico, from the Rocky Mountains to the Pacific Ocean. A subspecies, the black-tailed deer, is found from Alaska to California in redwood and fir forests.

Black-tailed deer

Mule deer

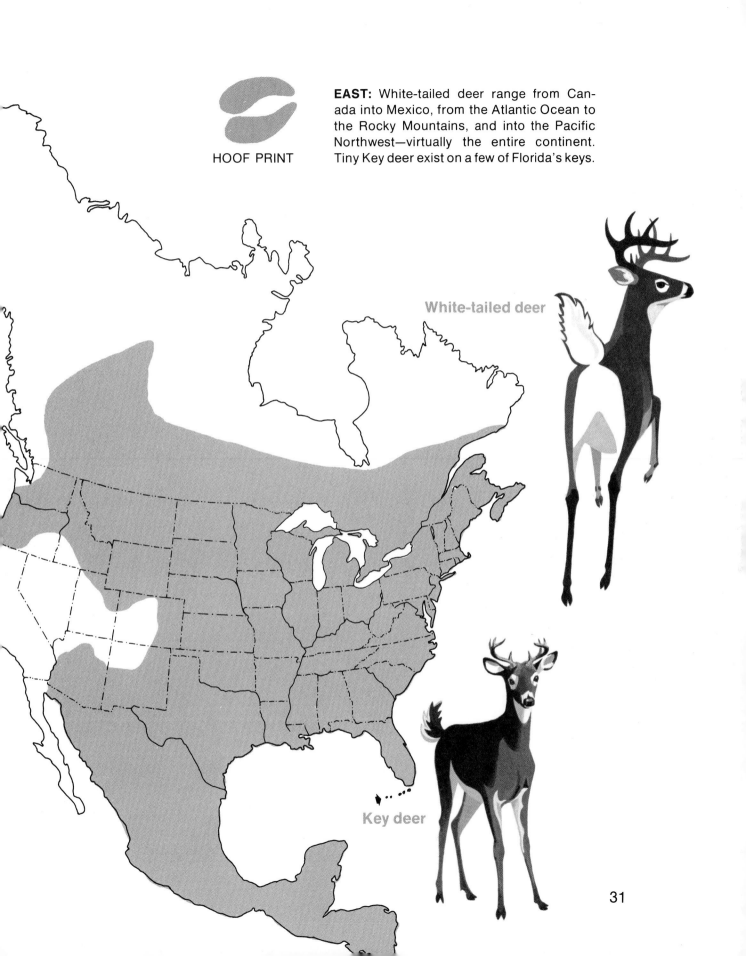

HOOF PRINT

EAST: White-tailed deer range from Canada into Mexico, from the Atlantic Ocean to the Rocky Mountains, and into the Pacific Northwest—virtually the entire continent. Tiny Key deer exist on a few of Florida's keys.

White-tailed deer

Key deer

31

WHEN YOU SEE A DEER . . .

Notice his alertness and curiosity as he looks over the area for danger. He has acute senses of sight, smell, and hearing. Make a sudden movement or sound and the deer will leap quickly away on nimble legs with his tail held erect, exposing the white underside. This flashing white banner is the mark of the white-tailed deer. Look at the beautiful white antlers and try to count the points. Your deer is a buck, for only male deer grow antlers. Observe his feet and look at his tracks. The deer walks and runs on two toes enclosed in hard hoofs.

The best time of day to see a deer is at sundown or sunrise. This is feeding time and he comes out of the woods to feed in orchards, pastures or grassy plains, or to drink water at the bank of a lake or river.

Watch particularly for deer at "Deer Crossing" signs. Man has learned that deer have favorite places for crossings. Deer pick areas that offer cover on both sides of the road—a heavy growth of trees or bushes or a protective gully. A quick leap across the road and he vanishes, out of danger. Some areas have concentrations of deer. Be alert in national and state parks, national forests and refuges, and other protected areas. Look carefully and you may glimpse a whitetail running free.

CREDITS

Leonard Lee Rue III white-tailed deer cover, pages 8, 9, 10, 11, 18, 19, 32; Thase Daniel 2-3; Hal H. Harrison 12-13; Tom Stack 14; John J. Dommers 15, 17; Joe Van Wormer, Bruce Coleman Inc. 16; James A. Collins 20; William A. Bake, Jr. 21; Wilford Miller 22; Lewis Wayne Walker 23; D. Hughes, Bruce Coleman Inc. 24; U. S. Fish and Wildlife Service 25; James H. Carmichael, Jr. back cover. Drawings by Frank Fretz 30-31.

NATIONAL WILDLIFE FEDERATION

Thomas L. Kimball	*Executive Vice President*
J. A. Brownridge	*Administrative Vice President*
James D. Davis	*Book Development*

Staff for This Book

EDITOR	Russell Bourne
ASSOCIATE EDITOR	Bonnie S. Lawrence
ART DIRECTOR	Donna M. Sterman
ART ASSISTANT	Ellen Robling
RANGER RICK ADVENTURES	J. A. Brownridge
	Robert Brownridge
RANGER RICK ART	Lorin Thompson
COPY EDITOR	Virginia R. Rapport
PRODUCTION AND PRINTING	Jim DeCrevel
	Mel M. Baughman, Jr.
CONSULTANT	Edwin Gould, Ph.D.
	The Johns Hopkins University

OUR OBJECTIVES

To encourage the intelligent management of the life-sustaining resources of the earth—its productive soil, its essential water sources, its protective forests and plantlife, and its dependent wildlife—and to promote and encourage the knowledge and appreciation of these resources, their interrelationship and wise use, without which there can be little hope for a continuing abundant life.